OVERLOOKED BIBLE CHARACTERS

OVERLOOKED BIBLE CHARACTERS
and the God Who Values People

DONNA L. HUISJEN

credo
house publishers

Published in the United States of America by Credo House Publishers,
a division of Credo Communications LLC, Grand Rapids, Michigan
credohousepublishers.com

ISBN: 978-1-62586-216-7

Cover and interior design by Believe Book Design

Printed in the United States of America
First edition

PREFACE

This short book is the second of three in the Characters of the Bible series, each containing twenty-five themed reflections on Bible persons. The first book in the series is *Flawed Bible Characters and the God Who Chooses, Uses, and Loves* and the third *Wicked Bible Characters and the God Who Works His Sovereign Plan*.

We know that God loves and values all people. What we don't know is whether he loves them all in a saving way. He longs for the salvation of all, but he leaves a big piece of the dynamic to us. We as Christians believe that salvation comes from a simple and straightforward action on our part—acceptance of his Son's ultimate sacrifice on our behalf and a sincere desire, henceforward, to live for, and to, him.

God's Word makes clear that he values unbelievers and uses them for his purpose and his glory. We don't understand how this can be, any more than we can work through our perception of unfairness when individuals never exposed to the gospel meet their end. We can only lean into God's all-encompassing, beyond-mind-boggling love for each and all of his image bearers and leave the outcomes to him.

You will notice that many of the characters considered in this volume were non-Israelites. Some, but not all, of them feared God, and some revealed goodness we find it difficult to account for, given their backgrounds and lack of knowledge. Why, we may ask regarding the seeming tangents and interludes in the ongoing story that introduce some of these diverse characters, did the authors see fit to include them in the Bible?

On perusing the table of contents, you may find that you don't recognize all of the names. Some of the characters represented are more obscure than others, but the Word has something to say to us by and through each of these accounts. Some of them tackle difficult stories, often glossed over or passed over as uncomfortable or even untouchable.

All of the characters considered in this book are portrayed in a positive, or mostly positive, light. All people are flawed, and these were certainly no exception, but their stories for the most part are brief and their characterizations limited. We Christians have a deep awareness of and sensitivity to sin, but we also rejoice in redemption, grace, and hope. These realities are present in and central to the outcomes of many of these stories. As for the others, we can't help but wonder at the residual goodness God allows in a fallen world.

CONTENTS

1

ABIGAIL

"David moved down into the Desert of Paran. A certain man in Maon, who had property
there at Carmel, was very wealthy. . . . His name was Nabal and his wife's name was Abigail. She was an intelligent and beautiful woman, but her husband was surly and mean
in his dealings."

1 Samuel 25:1–3

"When Abigail saw David, she quickly got off her donkey and bowed before David with
her face to the ground. She fell at his feet and said: . . . 'Please pay no attention, my lord,
to that wicked man Nabal. He is just like his name—his name means Fool, and folly goes
with him. And as for me, your servant, I did not see the men my lord sent.'"

1 Samuel 25:23–25

"When David heard that Nabal was dead, he said, 'Praise be to the LORD, who has upheld
my cause against Nabal for treating me with contempt. He has kept his servant from
doing wrong and has brought Nabal's wrongdoing down on his own head.' Then David
sent word to Abigail, asking her to become his wife."

1 Samuel 25:39

Pertinent Scripture: **1 Samuel 25**

❦

A Mexican proverb has it that "the house does not rest upon the ground, but
upon a woman." Our impression of ancient women typically centers around
subservience, but the Old Testament is full of stories in which women take the
upper hand. There are those who, like Jezebel and Zeresh (Haman's wife in the
book of Esther), push already wicked husbands into more overt evil. And those
like Rebekah who manipulate from behind the scenes, in her case taking advantage of a husband's cluelessness. The little-known story on which we focus today
features a capable and godly wife who intervenes to cover the sin of an out-of-
control husband.

"If you want to get across an idea," counsels Ralph Bunche, "wrap it up in
person." This was Abigail's approach in engaging David following her husband's
potentially costly gaffe. The point could be made that this remarkable woman was

the ultimate diplomat, but I prefer to see her in a slightly softer light, as peace-maker extraordinaire. Abigail's decisive action, taken in the interest not of subverting her husband but of protecting and even preserving her household, averted what could have lived on in history as a serious blight on David's character.

In terms of David's wives, we hear more about Michal and Bathsheba, both of whose stories include scandal. To set the stage for the Abigail story, it happened after Saul had given his daughter Michal, David's wife, to another husband (1 Samuel 25:44) but some time before David's indiscretion with Bathsheba (2 Samuel 11). Abigail takes her place in memory as the behind-the-scenes encourager and centering influence David needed to maintain balance.

Pause to consider the lovely imagery—an idiomatic expression found elsewhere in the Old Testament—in the italicized words to follow, spoken by Abigail to David: *"The life of my lord will be bound securely in the bundle of the living* by the LORD your God" (1 Samuel 25:29). What thoughts or feelings does this metaphor call up for you?

Little else is recorded about Abigail, but she does enter the story again in 1 Samuel 27:3 and in chapter 30, in which David's two wives, Abigail and Ahinoam, and his sons and daughters are taken captive in an Amalekite raid and later rescued by David and his men. We read that, when David learns of the loss of his family, he and his men weep aloud until they have no more strength for tears. A to-the-point comment assures us that all will be well: "But David found strength in the LORD his God." We can only surmise that Abigail found the same strength.

2

ABISHAG

"When King David was very old, he could not keep warm even when they put covers over him. So his attendants said to him, 'Let us look for a young virgin to serve the king and take care of him. She can lie beside him so that our lord the king may keep warm.' Then they searched throughout Israel for a beautiful young woman and found Abishag, a Shunammite, and brought her to the king. The woman was very beautiful; she took care of the king and waited on him, but the king had no sexual relations with her."

1 Kings 1:1–4

Pertinent Scripture: **1 Kings 1:1–2:25**

꙳

As English alphabetical order would have it, we find three reflections related to David clumped together near the front of this book. In this case, the time frame is David's last days on earth.

The use of a human body–that of a vibrant young woman, no less–to keep an old man warm sounds suspect in our ears, but there's beauty in it too. The author's presentation of Abishag is nothing but positive. Her loyalty to her lord, the king, is unquestioned. Abishag wasn't serving the aged king in an aloof, duty-motivated manner. David in his final days was undoubtedly no longer attractive. As a dedicated and caring nurse, Abishag was evidently able to overcome her natural revulsion at the sight of the wasted old man or at his involuntary sounds and smells. But she did so much more, nestling close to him in an effort to transfer some of her overflowing warmth and vitality.

Old age, like any other life passage, has its stages, of varying duration based on the individual's physical, mental, and emotional circumstances. This final stage, which we might associate with a lingering death, is no longer about the person's attitudes or choice of activity. The primary players in these final months or minutes are his or her caregivers. As our own loved ones face their final earthly passage, we can, if cast in a caregiving role, make all the difference in the quality of the experience–for them, for us, and even for our watching children.

"Now Adonijah . . . went to Bathsheba. . . . 'As you know,' he said, 'the kingdom was mine. All Israel looked to me as their king. But things changed, and the kingdom has gone to my brother; for it has come to him from the LORD. Now I have one request to make of you. . . . Please ask King Solomon . . . to give me Abishag the Shunammite as my wife.' . . . [Bathsheba said to Solomon], 'Let Abishag the Shunammite be given in marriage to your brother Adonijah.' King Solomon answered his mother, 'Why do you request Abishag the Shunammite for Adonijah? You might as well request the kingdom for him—after all, he is my older brother.' . . . Then King Solomon swore by the LORD: 'May God deal with me, be it ever so severely, if Adonijah does not pay with his life for this request.'"

1 Kings 2:13, 15–17, 21–23

Adonijah's request sounded innocent enough to Bathsheba, but Solomon rightly understood his older brother's ploy as a second attempt to gain the throne. Although Abishag remained a virgin, she would have been widely regarded as belonging to David's harem—possession of which would be viewed as signifying right of succession. In the ancient Near East, wives and concubines were typically passed down as property to a king's heir. No further mention is made of Abishag, but it is conjectured that she became a part of Solomon's harem.

This young woman was recruited into what was clearly a no-win situation. She made the best of it, fulfilling her expected role with strength and kindness. "Caregiving," observes Tia Walker, "often calls us to lean into love we didn't know possible." And Mason Cooley comments, "Compassion brings us to a stop, and for a moment we rise above ourselves." These outcomes are ideal rather than guaranteed, but they do provide a healthy perspective with which all of us can approach life prior to the passage of an elderly individual.

A selfless servant? A pawn? Abishag's choice (if she had one) entailed both; she must have had the foresight to understand the ramifications of her coming role change following the king's death. About one choice we do know: Abishag opted to follow through on her commitment, not grudgingly or minimally but with dignity and compassion. She served as a willing friend to David, whom Scripture calls God's friend (James 2:23)—perhaps we can declare, by extension, that she, too, was a friend of God!

3

BARZILLAI

"Barzillai the Gileadite also came down from Rogelim to cross the Jordan with the king [David] and to send him on his way from there. Now Barzillai was very old, eighty years of age. He had provided for the king during his stay in Mahanaim, for he was a wealthy man. The king said to Barzillai, 'Cross over with me and stay with me in Jerusalem, and I will provide for you.' But Barzillai answered the king, 'How many more years will I live, that I should go up to Jerusalem with the king? I am now eighty years old. Can I tell the difference between what is enjoyable and what is not? Can your servant taste what he eats and drinks? Can I still hear the voices of the male and female singers? Why should your servant be an added burden to my lord the king?'"

2 Samuel 19:31–35

Pertinent Scriptures: **2 Samuel 17:27–29; 19:31–38**

🌱

The setting is the return of David and his army to Jerusalem following Absalom's revolt and death. The mood of the army is somber, the men taking their cue from David to subdue their victory celebration while he mourns his son's loss. The party returning with David has reached the Jordan, and a contingent from Jerusalem has crossed the river to meet them at its bank.

Inclusion of this exchange between David and Barzillai feels random. We wonder why the author chose to record this tangent in his account. But this story has come down to us for a reason. Barzillai, a noble character, has done nothing particularly outstanding, but he has faithfully provided for the king during his unplanned absence from the palace. The appreciation between the two aging men is clearly mutual.

Old age, so significant a life passage, is a focus of much of the end of 2 Samuel, and this interlude takes up the theme. We're aware of the irony that some people become embittered with the diminishing effects of age, while others mellow. "Remember your Creator in the days of your youth," invites the Teacher in Ecclesiastes, "before the days of trouble come and the years approach when you will say, 'I find no pleasure in them'" (Ecclesiastes 12:1).

Some aging individuals grapple for a return to the past. Barzillai, recognizing the futility of this approach, has reverted to despair, rejecting any future prospect of pleasure or purpose. Some revel in the now. I can't help but contrast the perspective of the eighty-year-old Barzillai with that of Jean Renoir: "The advantage of being eighty years old is that one has had many people to love." Still others transition with age to an eager hope for a glorious forever fast approaching: "If the infinity of the sea may call out thus," muses Henryk Sienkiewicz, "perhaps when a man is growing old, calls come to him, too, from another infinity still darker and more deeply mysterious; and the more he is wearied by life the dearer are those calls to him."

Grief for the elderly is progressive, with individual and family losses coming incrementally but inevitably. For the fortunate believer who opts for a heightened sense of God's presence, along with ever more vibrant faith and hope, homesickness can gradually shift its direction. The beauty for us as Christians is that it's often God's face in those waning years we yearn most to see.

First Kings 2:1–19 details the dying David's charge to Solomon, in which the king systematically takes care of the business of succession with regard to Solomon's treatment of various individuals. Barzillai has evidently already died, but David has not forgotten the family of his supporter. "Show kindness to the sons of Barzillai of Gilead and let them be among those who eat at your table," he instructs his heir. "They stood by me when I fled from your brother Absalom."

The question occurs to us what we can learn from the inclusion of Barzillai in Old Testament history. Perhaps three things: a poignant treatise on God's concern for the aged; a call to everyday, behind-the-scenes generosity; and a reminder to appreciate those in our lives who reflect God's kindness through their actions. Barzillai, an old man who considered himself beyond usefulness, held an enduring place in David's heart for his faithful role during a trying time.

4

Boaz

"Ruth the Moabite said to Naomi, 'Let me go to the fields and pick up the leftover grain behind anyone in whose eyes I find favor.' Naomi said to her, 'Go ahead, my daughter.' So she went out, entered a field and began to glean behind the harvesters. As it turned out, she was working in a field belonging to Boaz, who was from the clan of Elimelek. . . . Boaz said to Ruth, 'My daughter, listen to me. Don't go and glean in another field and don't go away from here. . . . I have told the men not to lay a hand on you. . . . I've been told all about what you have done for your mother-in-law since the death of your husband. . . . May you be richly rewarded by the LORD, the God of Israel, under whose wings you have come to take refuge.'"

Ruth 2:1–3, 8–9, 11–12

Pertinent Scripture: **Ruth 2:1–4:12**

❦

Note the contrast between the behavior, attitudes, and godliness of the characters in this lyrical story and those depicted throughout most of Judges, which covers the same time period. There is some hint of the darker reality in Naomi's warning that her daughter-in-law might be taken advantage of in a field other than that of Boaz. We aren't told during whose judgeship these events occurred, but the story reassures us that God had not abandoned the faithful among his people. Bethlehem, the setting for the opening of the story of the Levite and his concubine in Judges 19:1–10 (a sobering read), seems to have been an enclave of civility in the midst of an uncertain world.

Though well aware of Boaz's identity and status in the community, Naomi does not instruct Ruth at the outset to glean in his field. This righteous woman is not about to take advantage of the good graces of a relative or to orchestrate events in her own favor; she allows God to lead but is ready to confirm Ruth's auspicious—though random—choice when she sees evidence of blessing.

It's important that we see in this chapter more than the lead-in to a romance. Boaz was probably not a "catch" for Ruth. An older but still virile relative of Ruth's deceased father-in-law, he is a man of God who perceives and rewards virtue in this hardworking, loyal young woman.

The sensitivity to notice and reward the value in others is a gift too seldom exercised in a self-centered world. We take our cue for doing so from the person and nature of the God whose image we bear—the same God who ascribes infinite worth to each person. In the words of Charles H. Percy, "Once we recognize the fact that every individual is a treasury of hidden and unsuspected qualities, our lives become richer, our judgment better, and our world is more right. It is not love that is blind, it is only the unnoticed eye that cannot see the real qualities of people."

Ruth's ritual enactment with Boaz in Ruth 3 seems brazen, but in the story's milieu this was the prescribed way for a woman to appeal to a relative's kinsman-redeemer obligation. Still, there can be little doubt this young woman followed through on her mother-in-law's instructions with trepidation.

Would Boaz have been making a personal sacrifice in marrying Ruth? Or would the opposite have been true? A case could be made for either, but the characters' feelings aren't shared. Charles Percy's point, above, about the blindness of love can take us in differing directions. An attraction based on the superficial can be visually impaired in terms of the ability to foresee painful realities to come. But an acuity of perception probing beneath the surface constitutes a deliberate blindness to the inconsequential and irrelevant. This is the eyes-wide-open quality of love that will stand and withstand—the kind of love made possible for us through our divine image bearing.

In Boaz and Ruth two individuals of unusual character and integrity were able to see beyond their external differences to form a strong union. And that character "gene" would be passed along through Obed to Jesse and ultimately to David. Much as God would later select an unassuming young girl to bear his Son, so in this earlier time he handpicked Ruth to bear Jesus's forebear.

It can be argued that the Boaz-Ruth connection might never have developed had not Naomi, Ruth, and Boaz, each in turn, taken the initiative to invite Providence to step in. Might God be waiting for a good-faith gesture on our part to introduce something into our lives that is beyond wonderful? Might he long to see evidence of our commitment *before* opening that next door?

5

THE CENTURION WITH THE SUFFERING SERVANT

"When Jesus had entered Capernaum, a centurion came to him, asking for help. 'Lord,' he said, 'my servant lies at home paralyzed, suffering terribly.' Jesus said to him, 'Shall I come and heal him?' The centurion replied, 'Lord, I do not deserve to have you come under my roof. But just say the word, and my servant will be healed. . . .' When Jesus heard this, he was amazed and said to those following him, 'Truly I tell you, I have not found anyone in Israel with such great faith. . . . Go! Let it be done just as you believed it would.'"

Matthew 8:5–8, 10, 13

Pertinent Scriptures: **Matthew 8:5–13; Luke 7:1–10**

❦

"A religious man," reflects Abraham J. Heshel, "is a person who holds God and man in one thought at one time, at all times, who suffers harm done to others, whose greatest passion is compassion, whose greatest strength is love and defiance of despair." I'm uncomfortable with the connotations of the term "religious." But beyond that, the description seems to fit this Roman centurion remarkably well. He informed Jesus not that his *valuable slave* was incapacitated and thus unable to perform his duties. No, his concern was for the *suffering man*. His stake in the situation was one human for another, not a master on behalf of his underling.

Nor did he, a Roman officer, approach this itinerant Jew with a superior attitude, expecting status-based service. Jesus, testing him, offered, "Shall I come and heal him?" He must have been caught off guard by the response: "Lord, I do not deserve to have you come under my roof. But just say the word, and my servant will be healed." The centurion, explaining his understanding of Jesus's authority, went on, "For I myself am a man under authority, with soldiers under me. I tell this one, 'Go,' and he goes; and that one, 'Come,' and he comes. I say to my servant, 'Do this,' and he does it."

This Roman may have been a God-fearer. Or he may have been impressed by the lifestyle he witnessed from Jesus's followers in Capernaum. The Jewish elders who come to Jesus on the centurion's behalf in Luke's version of the story commend him for loving the Jewish nation and for having built the Capernaum synagogue. But the distinction between Jew and Gentile in terms of Jesus's ministry and message was understood by all. The centurion comprehended that the merest request on his part for healing was presumptuous. Beyond the officer's other commendable qualities, it was the boldness of his faith that moved Jesus to action in this, his first remote healing.

The centurion's simple clause "I do not deserve . . ." doesn't strike us—until we learn that it is the same wording in the Greek as John the Baptist's "I am not worthy" in Matthew 3:11. John, the Jewish forerunner of Jesus, declared that he was unqualified even to carry Jesus's sandals! Both men implicitly understood their status in relation to the Healer.

In Luke's version of the story, the centurion does not approach Jesus himself but sends "some elders of the Jews," who plead with Jesus on his behalf: "This man deserves to have you do this, because he loves our nation and has built our synagogue." Notice here the declaration that the centurion does indeed "deserve" Jesus's services! Once Jesus nears the house in Luke's recollection of events, the centurion sends friends to meet him. It is through them that he vicariously declares his unworthiness: "Lord, don't trouble yourself, for I do not deserve to have you come under my roof. That is why I did not even consider myself worthy to come to you." How interesting that the friends do not insinuate that the centurion considered himself too important to bother to come himself on behalf of a mere slave!

We learn that Jesus was "amazed" by the centurion's faith. The Greek word translated "amazed" is used only twice in the Gospel accounts. Ironically, in the other instance Jesus is astounded by the Jews' *lack of faith*. Jesus, visiting his hometown of Nazareth, found only skepticism: "Jesus said, 'A prophet is not without honor except in his own town, among his relatives and in his own home.' He could not do any miracles there, except lay his hands on a few sick people and heal them. He was amazed at their lack of faith" (Mark 6:4–6).

This theme is repeated in the Gospel accounts when other believing Gentiles come to seek assistance from Jesus (see the chapter on the Syrophoenician woman). In both cases Jesus seems reluctant to deviate from his mission to the Jews and asks leading questions ("Shall I come . . . ?" in the centurion's account) to verify the level of faith. We almost sense a stalling technique! The testimonies of both of these Gentiles (the powerful centurion and the lowly mother) astonished Jesus! I can't help but suspect that they invigorated him, too.

6

CORNELIUS

"At Caesarea there was a man named Cornelius, a centurion in what was known as the Italian Regiment. He and all his family were devout and God-fearing; he gave generously to those in need and prayed to God regularly. One day at about three in the afternoon he had a vision. He distinctly saw an angel of God, who came to him and said, 'Cornelius! . . . Your prayers and gifts to the poor have come up as a memorial offering before God. Now send men to Joppa to bring back a man named Simon who is called Peter.'"

Acts 10:1–5

Peter "arrived in Caesarea. Cornelius was expecting them and had called together his relatives and close friends. As Peter entered the house, Cornelius met him and fell at his feet in reverence. . . . Peter went inside and found a large gathering of people. He said to them: 'You are well aware that it is against our law for a Jew to associate with or visit a Gentile. But God has shown me that I should not call anyone impure or unclean.'"

Acts 10:23–28

"Peter began to speak: 'I now realize how true it is that God does not show favoritism but accepts from every nation the one who fears him and does what is right. You know the message God sent to the people of Israel, announcing the good news of peace through Jesus Christ, who is Lord of all. . . . He commanded us to preach to the people and to testify that he is the one whom God appointed as judge of all the living and the dead.'"

Acts 10:34–36, 42

"Peter said, 'Surely no one can stand in the way of their being baptized with water. They have received the Holy Spirit just as we have.'"

Acts 10:46–47

Pertinent Scripture: **Acts 10**

❧

This pivotal story is a turning point in the New Testament—and in the salvation story. It provides closure to the reflection about the Roman centurion we have just considered and allows us Gentile Christians to exhale a sigh of relief. This centurion—like the one presented in the previous chapter; the one who proclaims Jesus the Son of God at the cross (Mark 15:39); and Julius of the imperial Regiment, who is kind to the prisoner Paul on the voyage to Rome (Acts 27)—appears in a totally positive light. Unlike the centurion with the suffering servant, though, this one is named. And unlike Jesus with his guarded response in the earlier story, Peter is here freed by the Holy Spirit to bring the gospel to Gentiles. Peter, who will spend the rest of his life still trying to reach the Jewish people, announces his equality with and to Cornelius: "Stand up. . . . I am only a man myself."

An excerpt from Wikipedia has this to say about the conversion of Cornelius and the baptism of his entire household, including family members, close friends, slaves, and possibly other affiliated persons: "The baptism of Cornelius is an important event in the history of the early Christian church, along with the conversion and baptism of the Ethiopian eunuch. The Christian church was first formed around the original disciples and followers of Jesus, all of whom, including Jesus himself, were Galilean, except for Judas, who was Judean. All males in the Judean community were Jews: they were circumcised and observed the Law of Moses. The reception of Cornelius sparked a debate among the leaders of the new community of followers of Jesus, culminating in the decision to allow Gentiles to become Christians without conforming to Jewish requirements for circumcision, as recounted in Acts 15."

The independent-minded Jewish people yearned for the overthrow of the Roman government, though many New Testament Roman officials are presented as honorable and fair-minded. Evidently many had spent their adult lives in Jewish communities and had come not only to tolerate but to admire the populace and even to love the nation, promote the religious institutions, and fear God—though they lacked an understanding of—or a feeling of entitlement to—inclusion in his salvation plan. In God's grace, he allowed his people to live in a stable and orderly empire with excellent roads and conditions eminently suited to the spread of the gospel. This provision from the God who loves all people benefited Jew and Gentile alike. This story provides an initial declaration of God's incredible inclusivity and serves as an emancipation proclamation for all of us Gentiles. It is worth celebration beyond what it typically evokes.

7

ELKANAH

"There was a certain man from Ramathaim, a Zuphite from the hill country of Ephraim, whose name was Elkanah. . . . He had two wives; one was called Hannah and the other Peninnah. Peninnah had children, but Hannah had none."

1 Samuel 1:1–2

"Whenever the day came for Elkanah to sacrifice, he would give portions of the meat to his wife Peninnah and to all her sons and daughters. But to Hannah he gave a double portion because he loved her, and the LORD had closed her womb."

1 Samuel 1:4–5

"Whenever Hannah went up to the house of the LORD, her rival provoked her till she wept and would not eat. Her husband Elkanah would say to her, 'Hannah, why are you weeping? Why don't you eat? Why are you downhearted? Don't I mean more to you than ten sons?'"

1 Samuel 1:7–8

"Samuel was ministering before the LORD—a boy wearing a linen ephod. Each year his mother made him a little robe and took it to him when she went up with her husband to offer the annual sacrifice. Eli would bless Elkanah and his wife, saying, 'May the LORD give you children by this woman to take the place of the one she prayed for and gave to the LORD.' Then they would go home. And the LORD was gracious to Hannah; she gave birth to three sons and two daughters."

1 Samuel 2:18–21

Pertinent Scripture: **1 Samuel 1:1–28**

❦

The opening to 1 Samuel reminds me. I'm reminded by the desolate Hannah of the emptiness in Sarai and Rebekah and Naomi and Elizabeth. More striking, though, is the similarity of this family constellation to that of Jacob, Leah, and Rachel.

Elkanah is clearly not the principal character in this drama. Much has been written of Hannah and Eli, and much more, of course, about Samuel. We know little about Peninnah, who comes off in the story as one-dimensional, in much the same way Leah before her did. But my intention in writing this book is to focus on some of the Bible's characters who are less in the forefront.

We see in Elkanah a faithful Israelite who clearly took his vows seriously—all of them, from his religious to his marriage vows. We see that he was fair-minded, and we know that he loved Hannah (we aren't told the same of Peninnah, though that issue is secondary to the account in 1 Samuel). We also surmise that Elkanah was nonconfrontational, avoiding conflict however he could, to the point of allowing Hannah to make up her own mind about dedicating their toddler to the Lord's service for his lifetime ("Do what seems best to you. Stay here until you have weaned him; only may the LORD make good his word"). Elkanah was in many ways shortsighted—as we all are—but he was never mean-spirited.

Elkanah's attempts to compensate Hannah for her childlessness unwittingly added fuel to Peninnah's jealous fire. His unapologetic preferential treatment of the obviously hurting Hannah, though well intentioned, only exacerbated the issue for the also hurting Peninnah, who longed above all else for evidence of her husband's love. An unknown author voiced the following: "Have they identified the gene that makes people pretend they're happy and that their life isn't a sham to compensate for broken dreams?" I selected this quote with Peninnah in mind. There seems to have been a whole lot of compensating going on! How sad that each of these dissatisfied women longed for precisely what the other had in plenty.

The hot box of polygamy aside, we may be compensating someone—one of our children, perhaps—for some disappointment, disability, or deficit. Our intention is to balance things out, to find a point of equilibrium in terms of contentment levels. But it seldom works that way; to begin with, we have no real idea of what's going on in each individual's heart of hearts. The successful, independent child may yearn for precisely the emotional "reward" the less competent sibling is reaping.

God is fully aware of the individual weaknesses of each of us. In the words of the psalmist David, "for he knows how we are formed, he remembers that we are dust" (Psalm 103:14). David had his own flaws—serious ones—but the God of love never ceased viewing him as his friend. How poignant that the same is true for each of us as we do our best in the situation God has occasioned for us.

8

EPHRON

"Abraham rose from beside his dead wife and spoke to the Hittites. He said, 'I am a foreigner and stranger among you. Sell me some property for a burial site here so I can bury my dead.' The Hittites replied to Abraham, 'Sir, listen to us. You are a mighty prince among us. Bury your dead in the choicest of our tombs. . . .' Abraham . . . said to them, 'If you are willing to let me bury my dead, then listen to me and intercede with Ephron son of Zohar on my behalf so he will sell me the cave of Machpelah, which belongs to him and is at the end of his field. Ask him to sell it to me for the full price of a burial site among you.' Ephron the Hittite was sitting among his people and he replied to Abraham in the hearing of all the Hittites who had come to the gate of his city. 'No, my lord,' he said. . . . 'I give you the field, and I give you the cave that is in it. I give it to you in the presence of my people. Bury your dead.'"

Genesis 23:3–6, 8–11

"Do not withhold good from those to whom it is due, when it is in your power to act."

Proverbs 3:27

Pertinent Scripture: **Genesis 23**

❦

Abraham, a resident alien who does not own land, insists upon paying for the field, and Ephron concedes that the land is worth four hundred shekels of silver, going on, "But what is that between you and me? Bury your dead.'" Abraham pays the going rate.

The Hittites were a people group descended from Heth, a third-generation descendant of Noah. They lived in Canaan, and the Israelites had ongoing relations with them, continuing through the post-exilic period (Ezra 9:1). Their religion was pluralistic, and their nature gods were often listed as witnesses to treaties and oaths. Due to their despicable pagan practices, the post-exodus Israelites were called upon to annihilate them (this did not happen) and the post-exilic Israelites to avoid intermarriage with them. Recall, however, that Uriah the Hittite, Bathsheba's first husband, who fought for David as one of his elite corps of Mighty Men, was a God-fearing Hittite of impeccable integrity.

15

As we see so frequently in Scripture, non-Israelites like Ephron responded to God's people with generosity. The universality of grief comes out strongly in this vignette. This shared human connection transcends the differences among people. Yes, Genesis 23 records respectful back-and-forth dialogue, but we get the impression that the mood was subdued. In times like this silence speaks resoundingly, to the point that little discussion is needed. Ram Dass observes, "We're fascinated by the words—but where we meet is in the silence between them."

It has been said that tears and laughter are the most universal of human experiences. Since all of us as humans are created in our Father's image and valued by him, we know that God relates to us in both situations. With regard to grief, we know that our tears are precious to him; the psalmist implores God in Psalm 56:8 to "record my misery; list my tears on your scroll—are they not in your record?" And Paul reminds us in Romans 8:26 that the Spirit intercedes for us with wordless groans when we don't know how to articulate our requests to the Father.

In these days of viral communication and global shrinking, the shared human experience of grief can quickly engulf the globe and overwhelm our psyches. Due in part to the continuous barrage of sensory and media input, we may conclude that our world is becoming steadily worse. But could this flood of fellowship, this global people-to-people bonding, be a manifestation of God's ameliorating grace? Could we humans, valued alike by our Creator, be becoming more and more a true global family?

A word of advice on Proverbs 3:27, quoted above, from GO InterNational speaks to each of us—as humans, not necessarily only as Christians: "Focusing on all of the world's problems at once can be overwhelming and cause us to think we can't make a difference. It is God's job to place specific people in our lives that need help, and it is also his job to give us the resources to help those people. We just need to be faithful to act in those moments with what he's given us, and we can let him take care of the rest!"

9

HATHAK

"When Mordecai learned of all that had been done, he tore his clothes, put on sackcloth and ashes, and went out into the city, wailing loudly and bitterly. . . . When Esther's eunuchs and female attendants came and told her about Mordecai, she was in great distress. . . . Esther summoned Hathak, one of the king's eunuchs assigned to attend her, and ordered him to find out what was troubling Mordecai and why."
Esther 4:1, 4–5

"Mordecai told him everything that had happened to him, including the exact amount of money Haman had promised to pay into the royal treasury for the destruction of the Jews. He also gave him a copy of the text of the edict for their annihilation . . . to show to Esther and explain it to her, and he told him to instruct her to go into the king's presence to beg for mercy and plead with him for her people."
Esther 4:7–8

"When Esther's words were reported to Mordecai, he sent back this answer: 'Do not think that because you are in the king's house you alone of all the Jews will escape. For if you remain silent at this time, relief and deliverance for the Jews will arise from another place. . . . And who knows but that you have come to your royal position for such a time as this?'"
Esther 4:12–14

Pertinent Scripture: **Esther 4:1–14**

❧

There is no God-talk in Esther, but his presence and providence permeate this lovely book.

We don't often think of extended families as reflecting personalities, but in contemplating our own, most of us could come up with a roughly consistent composite profile. We wouldn't ordinarily think of identifying family traits from a sampling of two, but Mordecai and Esther seem to have been all there were. A winning combination of modesty, loyalty, and courage melded with caution, impeccable timing, and sound judgment–these traits, reflected in "father" and "daughter"–worked together to make this nontraditional adoptive family ideal candidates for the physical salvation of the Jews in Persia.

17

We don't know the age difference between the two (or whether they were first cousins or more distant relatives)—only that Mordecai was a third-generation exile and that the roughly seventy years of captivity had run their course.

Prior to the filing of Haman's edict, Esther had at Mordecai's request informed no one in the Persian court of her lineage. Hathak, a eunuch (a castrated man placed in charge of a harem) assigned to attend to Esther's needs, may have been taken aback by Mordecai's revelation. If so, he expressed no surprise, nor did he pass this sensitive information to anyone else, subvert or modify the dialogue he carried between Esther and Mordecai, or betray their trust. There is no indication that Mordecai and Esther trusted Hathak as a risky last resort; his loyalty and trustworthiness seem not to have been in question.

Hathak and Haman, both Persians, the one a low-level palace official and the other a nobleman, serve as foils for one another in this intriguing story. Hathak is absolutely trustworthy, while Haman is the epitome of evil. Hathak's cooperation, taken for granted, was a necessary providential link in the salvation of the Jews who remained in Persia at this point in history.

God's valuation of this intermediary is never in question. How often in biblical accounts, as well as in our own stories, doesn't God intervene through the goodness of unbelievers? We do well to bear in mind that the God who loves all people is involved in the lives of each of his image bearers.

10

HIRAM

"There were peaceful relations between Hiram and Solomon, and the two of them made a treaty."

1 Kings 5:12

Hiram wrote to Solomon, "'I am sending you Huram-Abi, a man of great skill, whose mother was from Dan and whose father was from Tyre. . . . He will work with your skilled workers and with those of my lord, David your father. Now let my lord send his servant the wheat and barley and the olive oil and wine he promised, and we will cut all the logs from Lebanon that you need and will float them as rafts by sea down to Joppa. You can then take them to Jerusalem.'"

2 Chronicles 2:13–16

"The craftsmen of Solomon and Hiram and workers from Byblos cut and prepared the timber and stone for the building of the temple."

1 Kings 5:18

Pertinent Scriptures: **1 Kings 5; 2 Chronicles 2:1–16**

⚜

The Bible frequently portrays unbelieving rulers and leaders in an excellent light, from Pharaoh of Egypt and Abimelek of Gerar in their interactions with Abraham (Genesis 12:10–20 and 20:1–18) to Nebuchadnezzar, Darius, and Cyrus of Babylon and Persia to various representatives of the Roman government in Paul's day. Among them is Hiram, the Phoenician king of Tyre, a friend and ally of both David and his son Solomon. Such rulers unknowingly acted as God's instruments, yes. But all of us encounter exemplary people in our lives or communities—people who manifest the traits we associate with godliness . . . without being godly! Second Chronicles 2:12 might make us think of Hiram as a believer: "Hiram added, 'Praise be to the LORD, the God of Israel, who made heaven and earth!'" It would seem that Hiram's acknowledgment of God as Creator would have been exclusive, but these words are more likely an example of diplomacy in acknowledging another nation's god.

The story, cobbled together in bits and pieces, contains an element of understated mystique. The Israelites, as landlubbers, were never comfortable with seafaring; this fear of the deep is exemplified in several Old Testament passages ("Deep calls to deep in the roar of your waterfalls," reflect the sons of Korah in Psalm 42:7. "All your waves and breakers have swept over me"). Yet we read in 1 Kings 10:22 that Solomon "had merchant ships at sea with the fleet of Hiram. Once every three years the merchant ships came bringing gold, silver, ivory, apes, and monkeys." This is a scene worth imagining!

One trouble spot is related in 1 Kings 9:11–13. The culprit here is Solomon, and it is worth noting that Hiram's response, though honest, is gracious: "King Solomon gave twenty towns in Galilee to Hiram king of Tyre, because Hiram had supplied him with all the cedar and juniper and gold he wanted. But when Hiram went from Tyre to see the towns that Solomon had given him, he was not pleased with them. 'What kind of towns are these you have given me, my brother?' he asked. And he called them the Land of Kabul [good for nothing], a name they have to this day." Interestingly, the account cuts off there. We can only assume that Hiram, after voicing his mild reproof, accepted this gift for what it was worth!

God, we know, has allowed a measure of residual goodness in unbelievers to make life tolerable for all in a sinful world. He has imprinted on each human heart a moral awareness, an innate ability to distinguish right from wrong, along with an inkling of the requirements of grace and civility needed for humans to get along. Not only that, but we know that he values all people and that all are created in his image. Hiram comes off in Scripture as a loyal, noble ally of David and Solomon, one whose cooperation and assistance were uncompromising and unconditional. Would that each of us would leave such a legacy!

11

Hobab

"When Moses was forty years old, he decided to visit his own people, the Israelites. . . . Moses thought that his own people would realize that God was using him to rescue them, but they did not. The next day Moses came upon two Israelites who were fighting. He tried to reconcile them by saying, 'Men, you are brothers; why do you want to hurt each other?' But the man who was mistreating the other pushed Moses aside and said, 'Who made you ruler and judge over us?' When Moses heard this, he fled to Midian, where he settled as a foreigner and had two sons."

Acts 7:23–29

"Now Moses said to Hobab son of Reuel the Midianite, Moses' father-in-law, 'We are setting out for the place about which the LORD said, "I will give it to you." Come with us and we will treat you well, for the LORD has promised good things to Israel. . . . You know where we should camp in the wilderness, and you can be our eyes.'"

Numbers 10:29, 31

Pertinent Scriptures: **Exodus 2:15–25; 18:1–27; Numbers 10:29–34**

❧

Moses appreciated family. Having left behind his adoptive mother, the Egyptian princess, when he was forty, he seems to have melded seamlessly with both his family of origin and his Midianite in-laws. The book of Exodus doesn't share detail of Moses's reunion with his birth siblings; we know only from the leadup to the exodus and the event itself that God chose Aaron and Miriam for special roles in the deliverance of his people.

The story of Moses's flight to Midian is summarized by Stephen in Acts 7. Exodus 2:15–25 covers in a grand sweep the second forty year period in Moses's long life. Moses's encounter at a well with the seven daughters of the Midianite priest Reuel (also called Jethro) leads to a marriage and a sudden lifestyle change for Moses, who spends the next four decades herding Reuel's sheep. Pause for a moment to consider the jolting culture shock this must have been for this palace-raised Egyptian "prince." In Moses's own words, "I have become a foreigner in a foreign land."

During the exodus journey, Moses's father-in-law and brother-in-law stood behind him, visiting him at Sinai (apparently at different times) with every intention of heading back to Midian when Israel undertook from there its first organized march. Jethro acted as a true father to his already eighty-year-old son-in-law (makes one wonder how close Moses and Jethro may have been in age!), and Moses accepted his gracious advice and honored him with a special dinner in the presence of God (Exodus 18:13–27) before seeing him on his way. Hobab evidently intended to return to Midian later on, before Israel departed Sinai.

Jethro had departed on the best of terms with his son-in-law, and Hobab expected to do the same. However, Hobab's lifelong familiarity with the region—including its climate and potential dangers—ideally credentialed him to act as a scout or guide, and he acceded to Moses's request to accompany his sister's adopted people on their march. Hobab's vast experience no doubt stood the travelers in good stead.

Moses wasn't one to take advantage of someone's potential worth. "If you come with us," he pledged, "we will share with you whatever good things the LORD gives us" (Numbers 10:32). And they did: note Judges 4:11, 14–24; 5:24–27, which speak of Hobab's descendants. It's interesting that the husband of Jael of Judges 4 was Heber the Kenite, who "had left the other Kenites, the descendants of Hobab, Moses's brother-in-law, and pitched his tent by the great tree in Zaanannim near Kedesh."

The Israelites were remarkably accepting of foreigners in their midst, often enfolding them as brothers and sisters. The genealogy of Jesus Matthew includes at the beginning of his Gospel (addressing a Jewish audience) includes three Gentile women, Tamar, Rahab, and Ruth. Might this be a nod to the reality that God's grace was from earliest times extended both to women and to foreigners?

I'm struck by the metaphor that Hobab served as the Israelites' eyes. The Old Testament is replete with stories of non-Israelites serving God's people in myriad ways. The Israelites were chosen, yes—but that statement is in itself incomplete; they were chosen by God as his representatives to bless the nations. Hobab was blessed by his association with Moses and the Israelites—and, providentially, proved an invaluable blessing to them!

12

HOSEA

"The word of the LORD that came to Hosea son of Beeri during the reigns of Uzziah, Jotham, Ahaz and Hezekiah, kings of Judah, and during the reign of Jeroboam son of Jehoash king of Israel: When the LORD began to speak through Hosea, the LORD said to him, 'Go, marry a promiscuous woman and have children with her, for like an adulterous wife this land is guilty of unfaithfulness to the LORD.' So he married Gomer."

Hosea 1:1–2

"The LORD said to me, 'Go, show your love to your wife again, though she is loved by another man and is an adulteress. Love her as the LORD loves the Israelites, though they turn to other gods.' So I bought her. . . . Then I told her, 'You are to live with me many days; you must not be a prostitute or be intimate with any man, and I will behave the same way toward you.'"

Hosea 3:1–2

Pertinent Scripture: **Hosea 1:1–3:5**

✣

Although Hosea hailed from the northern kingdom of Israel, he most likely wrote from Judah after the fall of Samaria, the northern capital. The historical portions of this book give an account of incredible obedience. As with the death of Ezekiel's wife, Hosea's marriage was used by God as an object lesson for his unfaithful people. It's difficult to fathom God's modus operandi in these cases. It has no equivalent in our lives, other than perhaps his call to take a path we might not have chosen. It is helpful for us to accept this account as historical truth and to bear in mind that Gomer and Hosea were multi-faceted, flesh-and-blood people who were not manipulated by God and were responsible for their own actions.

A quote from Jennifer Egan may begin to capture the motivation of Gomer: "Her only thought was of getting away, as if she were carrying a live grenade from inside the house, so that when it exploded, it would destroy just herself." We have no real idea how Gomer felt or what torments drove her. There can be little doubt, though, that she was hurting and conflicted. Of Hosea's feelings we know nothing.

On a literal level, you or I wouldn't knowingly unite with a morally loose or difficult spouse, but it's possible to find ourselves in a marital relationship very different from what we had anticipated. When we take our vows seriously, we try to do whatever it takes to make the union work. Our hurt may stretch into long suffering—longer than we imagined ourselves capable of enduring. We may have to stack forgiveness on forgiveness, finally achieving a less than comfortable truce.

> "Come, let us return to the LORD. He has torn us to pieces but he will heal us; he has injured us but he will bind up our wounds. . . . Let us acknowledge the LORD; let us press on to acknowledge him."
>
> Hosea 6:1, 3

A more universal application of Hosea comes in the book's lengthier poetic sections. The theme of punishment of a rebellious people is not part of our story, but we, like Hosea, live in trying times that can involve difficult choices. While God is never the author of evil, he does allow it in our lives, though his loving purpose is always transcendent (Romans 8:28).

This true story had application for the Old Testament Israelites, but its symbolism goes much further for us who live in the new covenant reality. Just as Hosea was willing to *purchase* back his degraded wife, so Christ has redeemed us from the consequences of sin. Hosea's call comes to us, too—not to acknowledge God in a casual manner but to *press on* to do so. The reward is more than worth the effort: after we press on to acknowledge him, we are invited to lean into his love.

13

ITTAI

"The king set out, with all the people following him, and they halted at the edge of the city. All his men marched past him, along with all the Kerethites and Pelethites; and all the six hundred Gittites who had accompanied him from Gath marched before the king. The king said to Ittai the Gittite, 'Why should you come along with us? Go back and stay with King Absalom. You are a foreigner, an exile from your homeland. You came only yesterday. And today shall I make you wander about with us, when I do not know where I am going? Go back, and take your people with you.'"

2 Samuel 15:17–20

"The foreigner residing among you must be treated as your native-born. Love them as yourself, for you were foreigners in Egypt. I am the LORD your God."

Leviticus 19:34

Pertinent Scripture: **2 Samuel 15:17–22**

❦

David's interactions with Ittai the Gittite (a Philistine) and Barzillai the Gileadite, both considered in this book, mirror each other. Both take place while David is traveling with his army and a huge entourage of supporters—back and forth on the same momentous journey—and both are interludes that feel random to us as readers. What we don't know upon first reading is that both of these individuals were important to David. This incident with Ittai occurs first, while David is fleeing Jerusalem following the coup by his son Absalom. In the second, involving Barzillai, David is returning following Absalom's death (2 Samuel 17:27–29).

In this story, David and his entourage are fleeing Jerusalem, and Ittai, a very recent émigré evidently conscripted by David for leadership in his army (see 2 Samuel 18:1, 5), along with his men and numerous families, is with him. In the second story Barzillai, an elderly Gileadite who has been David's benefactor during his displacement, returns with him as far as the Jordan River.

In the present account, Ittai declines David's invitation to return to the relative safety of Jerusalem, staunchly marching along beside the king in his flight. Later, on David's return trek, Barzillai, in light of his advanced age, declines the king's invitation to cross the Jordan with the large assemblage to begin a new life in Jerusalem under David's care.

David's comment that Ittai had come to Jerusalem "only yesterday" is probably idiomatic or at least exaggerated. Ittai's response reminds me of Ruth's reply to Naomi a few generations earlier when Naomi invited her Moabite daughter-in-law to return to her homeland rather than accompany an old, desolate woman to Bethlehem (ironically, on the outskirts of Jerusalem): "Don't urge me to leave you or to turn back from you. Where you go I will go, and where you stay I will stay. Your people will be my people and your God my God" (Ruth 1:16)

These traveling stories together provide a fascinating glimpse into life in this early period of Israel's leadership. All three accounts (those of Ruth, Ittai, and Barzillai) feature remarkable loyalty on the part of foreigners, coupled with surprising inclusivity from the Israelite nation—and from God. This motif is repeated again and again throughout the Old Testament.

Nearly all of us in North America come from immigrant stock, and the argument can be made that our melding together, despite the inevitable problems, has resulted in unique strength and mutual resolve. We can take our cue for acceptance and tolerance from God's ready incorporation of aliens into full membership in his chosen race from its earliest beginnings. "History shows," observes Claudio Magris, "that it is not only senseless and cruel, but also difficult to state who is a foreigner."

14

JEHOIADA AND JEHOSHEBA

Ahaziah "followed the ways of the house of Ahab, for his mother encouraged him to act wickedly. He did evil in the eyes of the LORD, as the house of Ahab had done, for after his father's death they became his advisers, to his undoing."
2 Chronicles 22:3–4

Pertinent Scriptures: **2 Chronicles 22:1–9; 23–24; 2 Kings 11:17–12:21**

❦

T he history of Israel and Judah, intertwined here through marriage, is difficult to follow. I'm including the cast of characters in the dramatic backstory of Joash and Jehoiada—you might want to read it twice. Judah's king Ahaziah was the son of Jehoram of Judah and Athaliah of Israel, the daughter of Ahab who had married Jehoram in a political alliance. Jehosheba, Jehoram's (and Athaliah's?) daughter and Ahaziah's sister, was married to the chief priest, Jehoiada. This couple secreted away Ahaziah's infant son, Joash, Jehosheba's nephew, at the time of Athaliah's massacre of Judah's royal family (we aren't told why Jehosheba was spared).

> "When Athaliah the mother of Ahaziah saw that her son was dead, she proceeded to destroy the whole royal family. But Jehosheba, the daughter of King Jehoram and sister of Ahaziah, took Joash son of Ahaziah and stole him away from among the royal princes, who were about to be murdered. . . . He remained hidden with his nurse at the temple of the LORD for six years while Athaliah ruled the land."
> 2 Kings 11:1, 3

The vignette from 2 Kings 11 is part of a complicated story told over the course of multiple chapters in 2 Kings and 2 Chronicles. This portion reads like a fairytale. It's difficult to fathom a controlling woman intending harm to her own children or grandchildren. Ahab's wife, Jezebel, and her daughter Athaliah are the consummate biblical equivalents of Disney's cast of Cruellas from so many stories featuring power-hungry women.

(As an aside, it's interesting to reflect on other instances in Scripture in which the life of an otherwise doomed infant was spared. Think of Moses, Mephibosheth, and Jesus. Through God's providence, none of these instances was random. Mephibosheth's rescue allowed David to keep a solemn promise to Jonathan. Pause to imagine the ramifications had either Moses or Jesus been included in an intended infant massacre!)

> "In the seventh year Jehoiada sent for the commanders . . . and the guards and had them brought to him at the temple of the LORD. He made a covenant with them and put them under oath at the temple of the LORD. Then he showed them the king's son. . . . [Joash] then took his place on the royal throne. All the people of the land rejoiced, and the city was calm, because Athaliah had been slain with the sword at the palace. Joash was seven years old when he began to reign."
> 2 Kings 11:4, 19–21

> "Joash did what was right in the eyes of the LORD all the years of Jehoiada the priest."
> 2 Chronicles 24:2

There is foreshadowing in the short sentence that comprises that last verse. Our hopes for little Joash run high. The account of the seven-year-old's ascension to the throne and his promising early years under the tutelage of his uncle is heartwarming. All is well until the old priest's death; it seems that the adage "out of sight, out of mind" defines Joash's heart-set and mindset after that. For whatever reason, Joash had failed to internalize the goodness he'd seen modeled in his uncle; once Jiminy Cricket slid down from his shoulder, his conscience ceased to operate.

An unknown author makes the following observation: "It should always be kept in mind that what you are after with your child is not that he should learn obedience but that he should learn to govern himself." It's important for us as parents to make certain our children at some point take over as arbiters of their own attitudes and behaviors.

The biblical authors do not fault Jehoiada or Jehosheba, both of whom functioned first as saviors and later as faithful servants to the divine cause, doing all they could to further the fulfillment of God's plan to continue David's line. Jehoiada may have been shortsighted–or the shortsightedness may have been Joash's–but this priest and his wife are presented in Scripture as loyal servants who received and passed along God's grace.

28

15

LOIS AND EUNICE

"These commandments that I give you today are to be on your hearts. Impress them on your children. Talk about them when you sit at home and when you walk along the road, when you lie down and when you get up."
Deuteronomy 6:6–7

"Paul, an apostle of Christ Jesus by the command of God our Savior and of Christ Jesus our hope, to Timothy my true son in the faith."
1 Timothy 1:1–2

"I am reminded of your sincere faith, which first lived in your grandmother Lois and in your mother Eunice and, I am persuaded, now lives in you also."
2 Timothy 1:5

"But as for you, continue in what you have learned and have become convinced of, because you know those from whom you learned it, and how from infancy you have known the Holy Scriptures, which are able to make you wise for salvation through faith in Christ Jesus."
2 Timothy 3:14–15

Pertinent Scriptures: 2 Timothy **1:1–14; 3:10–17**

꧁꧂

"**P**aul came to Derbe and then to Lystra," writes Luke is Acts 16:1, "where a disciple named Timothy lived, whose mother was Jewish and a believer but whose father was a Greek." We don't know much about Timothy's father, including the degree to which he was involved with his son, but he was evidently uninterested in the things of God. It's probable that Timothy, still quite young, was an obvious candidate for a spiritual father figure—a need Paul intuited and filled, taking him under his wing as he and Silas moved on from Lystra.

Lois and Eunice had faithfully raised young Timothy in the Jewish faith, though both had recently converted to Christianity. Matriarchal faith transmission is, as we know, a significant factor in many churches today in which faith-filled and faithful moms are carrying the bulk of responsibility for their children's nurture.

Authors Kimberly Morgan and Sally Steenland offer provocative thoughts on the role of the church in helping to sustain mom-based families: "As women (and men) increasingly grapple with shifting gender roles and responsibilities, as families face greater economic stress, and as women juggle multiple tasks in days that are too short, religious institutions can provide sustenance and support. . . . They need to provide . . . a moral vision that values women and family in a way that is neither regressive nor nostalgic, but authentic and prophetic for today."

It is helpful to remember that, so early in church history, no generation had yet been raised in the Christian faith from infancy. But Timothy's knowledge of the Old Testament Jewish Scriptures prepared him to recognize Christ as their fulfillment. In the words of C. S. Lewis, "The world does not consist of 100 percent Christians and 100 percent non-Christians. There are people (a great many of them) who are slowly ceasing to be Christians but who still call themselves by that name: some of them are clergymen. There are other people who are slowly becoming Christians though they do not yet call themselves so." These numbers include children of believing parents who are engaged in the work of internalizing what they have been taught, coming to their own conclusions, and making their own commitments. Timothy owed a debt of gratitude for the spiritual father who played such an important role in his maturation in the faith, but this stage of his faith life wouldn't have been possible without the early influences of a committed mother and grandmother.

16

LYDIA

"We [Paul, Luke, Timothy, and Silas] traveled to Philippi, a Roman colony and the leading city of that district of Macedonia. . . . On the Sabbath we went outside the city gate to the river, where we expected to find a place of prayer. We sat down and began to speak to the women who had gathered there. One of those listening was a woman from the city of Thyatira named Lydia, a dealer in purple cloth. She was a worshiper of God. The Lord opened her heart to respond to Paul's message. When she and the members of her household were baptized, she invited us to her home. 'If you consider me a believer in the Lord,' she said, 'come and stay at my house.' And she persuaded us."

Acts 16:12–15

"Be devoted to one another in love. Honor one another above yourselves. Never be lacking in zeal, but keep your spiritual fervor, serving the Lord. Be joyful in hope, patient in affliction, faithful in prayer. Share with the Lord's people who are in need. Practice hospitality."

Romans 12:10–13

Pertinent Scripture: **Acts 16:11–15**

❦

Social responsibility for Christians dictated first the care of family. In Paul's words, "Anyone who does not provide for their relatives, and especially for their own household, has denied the faith and is worse than an unbeliever" (1 Timothy 5:8). But Paul took the mandate further, calling upon believing families and householders to throw open their doors to other Christians: "As we have opportunity, let us do good to all people, especially to those who belong to the family of believers" (Galatians 6:10).

Our Lord wants us to reflect his love and grace indiscriminately, yet Christ has a special, protective love for his own. At the very least, when it comes to extending hospitality, we aren't to overlook others in Christ's kingdom family. How slow we can be at times to set aside cultural and other differences to fully accept and trust one another.

Lydia may have been a Jew, but it is more likely that she was a Gentile worshiper of God who followed the Old Testament moral law and had affiliated with the very small Jewish community in and around Philippi. She herself, a business-woman identified as a "dealer in purple cloth," was originally from Thyatira, a city famous for its dyeing works. Since Philippi evidently lacked the quorum of ten men necessary for the erection of a synagogue, Jewish women—and possibly other God-fearing Gentiles—were in the habit of sitting by the Gangites River bank outside the city gates for prayer.

Lydia, whom we can imagine was painfully aware of her status as a Gentile, not to mention a woman, must have felt some trepidation in offering lodging to these male travelers. She had nothing to fear, yet how sad that she felt the need to question whether the apostle considered her a believer! A newly minted Christian who immediately took the step of having herself and her household baptized, her intent was clearly to offer the freedom, undisturbed by dividing lines, of which Henri J. M. Nouwen speaks: "Hospitality means primarily the creation of free space where the stranger can enter and become a friend instead of an enemy. . . . It is not to bring men and women over to our side, but to offer freedom not disturbed by dividing lines." The Christian faith made possible radical societal changes, and the Holy Spirit's irresistible urging was already instrumental in Lydia's heart. Though drawn to the Jewish faith, she had never felt compelled to convert to Judaism, but Paul's good news was altogether different.

It is significant to recognize that Lydia takes her place as the first Christian convert on the European continent. As Herbert Lockyer notes, "Lydia always had 'open house' for the saints of God and her home became a center of Christian fellowship in Philippi with perhaps the first Christian church being formed therein. When Paul came to write his letter to the Philippians, we can rest assured that Lydia was included in all the saints at Philippi to whom he sent his salutations (Philippians 1:1–7); and was also in his mind as one of those women who labored with him in the Gospel (Philippians 4:3)."

17

Naaman's Servant Girl

"Now Naaman was commander of the army of the king of Aram. He was a great man in the sight of his master and highly regarded, because through him the Lord had given victory to Aram. He was a valiant soldier, but he had leprosy. Now bands of raiders from Aram had gone out and taken captive a young girl from Israel, and she served Naaman's wife. She said to her mistress, 'If only my master would see the prophet who is in Samaria. He would cure him of his leprosy.'"

2 Kings 5:1–2

"How can we sing the songs of the Lord while in a foreign land? If I forget you, Jerusalem, may my right hand forget its skill. May my tongue cling to the roof of my mouth if I do not remember you, if I do not consider Jerusalem my highest joy."

Psalm 137:4–6

Pertinent Scripture: **2 King 5:1–6**

❦

I'm struck by three things in the verses from 2 Kings, above. First, the declaration that the Lord had given victory to Aram takes the reader by surprise. The text doesn't note victory over *whom,* but we do see unexpected evidence of God's work on behalf of unbelievers, including non-Israelite nations. Second, we find it surprising that Naaman, despite his leprosy, continued to function in his role as military commander. Most surprisingly, we see the unexpected concern of a captive slave over her master's condition.

Moses had clearly delineated to a new generation of Israelites following the forty years in the wilderness the curses for disobedience, including this: "Your sons and daughters will be given to another nation, and you will wear out your eyes watching for them day after day, powerless to lift a hand" (Deuteronomy 28:32). Second Kings 5:2 speaks of one such young girl who had been swooped up and carried away by Aramean raiders.

The Bible is replete with the wistful and wishful expressions of God's people, often prefaced with sighs like "If only . . ." or "Oh, that . . ." Young people are resilient, and we have no reason to suspect that Naaman or his wife had mistreated this girl. Still, it seems amazing that she cared so deeply about the well-being of her master!

Daniel Long rightly asserts that our mature ability and inclination to love are byproducts of our early experience with the love of family: "So much of what is best in us is bound up in our love of family, that it remains the measure of our stability because it measures our sense of loyalty. All other pacts of love or fear derive from it and are modeled upon it." By all appearances this servant girl was motivated by love, not fear.

Following are excerpts from Herbert Lockyer's study of this servant girl:

> The home from which she was forcibly taken was a godly Hebrew one in which God was honored, and His servant, Elisha, was revered. Young though the maid was, she feared the Lord and her incorrigible faith was a flame lighting the spirit of every other person in the drama. Naaman and his wife, the Syrian king, the servants who quickened Naaman's spirit, and the prophet Elisha himself, all felt the impact of a little maid who was wholly the Lord's and believed implicitly in His power. Brought to live among idolaters, she clung to her own faith in the living God and sought to share her knowledge of Him with others. Hers was a strong, contagious faith, enabling her to live without any feeling of homesickness in an alien land, and any resentment against her captors. Her love for God inspired her to love her masters and to win her way into their affection and confidence. . . .
>
> The maid might have noticed how the incurable disease was preying upon the mind and body of her kind master. This shadow over the household gave the maid her opportunity, and having learned to sing the song of the Lord in a strange land, she was ready to tell her distressed mistress that her husband could be cured.

An element of that learned love mentioned by Daniel Long too often falls between the cracks as we push our children in the direction of ever-expanding knowledge and skill sets in a competitive and often unkind world. That element is compassion. It's a quality, a force, a gift that needs to be nurtured and extended beyond the confines of family (though it begins there) in a wide and generous swathe of concern for humanity, both individually and as a whole. Compassion is intrinsic to the way we as Christ-followers reflect and disperse our Lord's love throughout a hurting world he so deeply values.

18

PETER'S MOTHER-IN-LAW

"As Jesus was walking beside the Sea of Galilee, he saw two brothers, Simon called Peter and his brother Andrew. They were casting a net into the lake, for they were fishermen. 'Come, follow me,' Jesus said, 'and I will send you out to fish for people.' At once they left their nets and followed him. Going on from there, he saw two other brothers, James son of Zebedee and his brother John. They were in a boat with their father Zebedee, preparing their nets. Jesus called them, and immediately they left the boat and their father and followed him."

Matthew 4:18–22

"Jesus left the synagogue and went to the home of Simon. Now Simon's mother-in-law was suffering from a high fever, and they asked Jesus to help her. So he bent over her and rebuked the fever, and it left her. She got up at once and began to wait on them."

Luke 4:38–39

"Each of you should use whatever gift you have received to serve others, as faithful stewards of God's grace in its various forms. . . . If anyone serves, they should do so with the strength God provides, so that in all things God may be praised through Jesus Christ."

1 Peter 4:10–11

Pertinent Scripture: **Luke 4:38–5:11**

❦

According to the sequence of Luke's Gospel, Jesus healed Simon Peter's mother-in-law (Luke 4:38–49) *before* he called the two sets of brothers to be his first disciples (5:1–11). But the order is reversed in Matthew and Mark, with the calling of the first four disciples and then the healing of Peter's mother-in-law shortly afterward. Either way, it is clear that Jesus was acquainted with these fishermen and that these two events happened within a short timeframe.

The hint of the family life of Simon Peter—quite likely similar to that of Andrew, James, and John and of at least some of the other disciples who were called later on—leaves intriguing questions. It is evident that Peter was at that time, or at least had been, married. When it comes to these two sets of brothers, partners in a small-scale fishing business, we wonder who was to take over during their itinerant years. Was Zebedee, the fisherman father of James and John, still fully active? What about Peter and Andrew's parents? Was Peter's father-in-law living? Were there children in the home? The Gospel writer doesn't say, nor do we need to know.

The response of Peter's mother-in-law says something not only about the radical nature of her healing but about her own nature. Service was evidently what this dear woman was all about. It came as naturally to her as breathing; it was the activity she was, in her own mind and heart, healed to resume. Most of us are acquainted with some relative, friend, or fellow church member who, despite continuing physical challenges, rises again and again for selfless service—and in some inexplicable way receives added strength and determination in the process.

There can be little doubt that profound gratitude motivated her as well. What did she have to offer this healer? Her service, from an overflowing heart. "Everybody can be great," asserted Dr. Martin Luther King Jr. "Because anybody can serve. You don't have to have a college degree to serve. You don't have to make your subject and verb agree to serve. You only need a heart full of grace. A soul generated by love."

I'm reminded by Peter's mother-in-law of Martha, another humble woman featured in the Gospels. Martha, like Peter's mother-in-law, was gifted in the area of hospitality and expressed her love and appreciation through serving. The story is told in Matthew 26:6–13 and John 12:1–8 of Martha's sister Mary (unnamed in Matthew) demonstrating her gush of gratitude for Jesus by pouring expensive perfume on his feet. Jesus calls this gesture a "beautiful thing." The contrast between these sisters is highlighted in Luke 10:38–42, where Martha's own "beautiful thing" is her outpouring of grateful hospitality. Paul enjoins his readers in Ephesians 6:7 to "serve wholeheartedly, as if you were serving the Lord, not people." Peter's mother-in-law literally served Jesus . . . and all others present with her Christlike hospitality.

19

PUBLIUS

"Once safely on shore, we found out that the island was called Malta. The islanders showed us unusual kindness. They built a fire and welcomed us all because it was raining and cold."

Acts 28:1–2

"There was an estate nearby that belonged to Publius, the chief official of the island. He welcomed us to his home and showed us generous hospitality for three days. His father was sick in bed, suffering from fever and dysentery. Paul went in to see him and, after prayer, placed his hands on him and healed him. When this had happened, the rest of the sick on the island came and were cured. They honored us in many ways; and when we were ready to sail, they furnished us with the supplies we needed. After three months we put out to sea in a ship that had wintered in the island."

Acts 28:7–11

Pertinent Scripture: **Acts 27:1–28:10**

⚜

The account of the storm and shipwreck shared by Luke in Acts 27 is riveting and sensory. I urge you to sit back and allow your imagination to sail. Paul, accompanied by Luke and under the authority of a centurion, is bound with other prisoners for a Roman prison. Contrary winds slow the ship's headway; it finally anchors in Fair Havens. Paul foresees disaster in terms of the fast-approaching winter, but the centurion, knowing this harbor to be unsuitable for wintering, follows the advice of the ship's pilot and owner and votes to press onward.

A gentle south wind seeming to bode well, the ship, carrying 276 souls, sets sail–only to be overtaken by a hurricane-force Northeaster. Envision the flimsy vessel, held together by ropes passed underneath its hull, being buffeted for many days with neither sun nor stars nor the luxury of opportunity for nourishment. Picture Paul buffering the courage of the beleaguered crew and passengers with the promise that all aboard will be saved.

Take the time to read the account of the shipwreck itself (Acts 27:27–44), allowing your mind to dwell on the details. Picture the sailors trying to sneak off in the lifeboat; the soldiers cutting the ropes to prevent this abandonment;

Paul urging all on board to take sustenance—their first food in two weeks; the ship running aground and breaking up; the soldiers planning to kill the prisoners to prevent their escape; the centurion thwarting this plan; and all aboard either swimming to floating on planks and arriving safely ashore.

Continue reading Acts 28:1–10. Feel on your shoulders the driving rain; sense on your hands the warmth of the bonfire; allow the cold, superstitious horror of the snake latching onto Paul's hand to wash over you; and experience the shock of the islanders when this Roman prisoner appears unscathed.

We can't help but wonder the reason for this interlude in the ongoing movement of the story, though we recognize the pause as a divine appointment. Paul and Publius had no prior knowledge of one another. But mutual understanding, a universal language, removed any barriers that might have gotten in their way. Paul refers in Romans 2:14–15 to the innate goodness often seen in nonbelievers, perhaps especially those who've never had an opportunity to hear the gospel message: "Indeed, when Gentiles, who do not have the law, do by nature things required by the law, they are a law for themselves. . . . They show that the requirements of the law are written on their hearts."

Compassion and hospitality to needy strangers seem to be intrinsic values around the world—a result of the residual goodness God has permitted the human race after the fall—except when underlying ethnic or other hostilities get in the way. I'm moved by a reflection from Thomas G. Long: "The stranger at the door is the living symbol and memory that we are all strangers here. . . . To show hospitality to the stranger is . . . to say, 'We are all beggars here together. Grace will surprise us both.'"

In this case the grace, from the human side, was presented by the unbeliever. The question comes to mind how well we as Christians stack up in the area of extending grace, hospitality, and healing to others, both the stranger and those closest to us (depending on our circumstances, either one can prove the more difficult). When we fall short in either area, a critical world is quick to take note.

We aren't told the responses of any of the varied cast of characters in this drama to the kindness extended by Paul, the centurion, or Publius and his fellow islanders. More importantly, we have no idea of the effect of the gospel message Paul must surely have shared during the intermission on Malta—on the centurion, the soldiers, the sailors, the prisoners, or the residents of Malta. What we do see clearly is evidence of God's love for people—people of all backgrounds and walks of life, each and all image bearers of the divine who may never have been apprised of their valued status in God's eyes. We do know that God wastes no opportunity to reach individuals and people groups with the message of his love.

20

REUEL (JETHRO)

> "One day, after Moses had grown up, he went out to where his own people were and watched them at hard labor. He saw an Egyptian beating a Hebrew. Looking this way and that and seeing no one, he killed the Egyptian and hid him in the sand. The next day he went out and saw two Hebrews fighting. He asked the one in the wrong, 'Why are you hitting your fellow Hebrew?' The man said, 'Who made you ruler and judge over us? Are you thinking of killing me as you killed the Egyptian?'"
>
> Exodus 2:11–14

Pertinent Scriptures: **Exodus 2:11–25; 18:1–27**

❦

Moses's lifetime divides neatly into contrasting thirds, each forty years in length. While Exodus 2:11 advises us only that Moses had grown up, Acts 7:23 clarifies that he was forty years old when he went out to visit the Israelites. Despite his privileged upbringing, he had not forgotten who he was.

It isn't surprising that the Israelites distrusted him. His flight from Pharaoh's wrath was immediate, and he traveled as he was (we read that Reuel's daughters recognized him as an Egyptian). In God's providence, he ended up at the home of the Midianite priest Reuel (also called Jethro), whose name means "friend of God."

Moses's adaptation to life as a family man and shepherd in what must have seemed primitive surroundings is remarkable. He named his older son Gershom, meaning "I have become a foreigner in a foreign land." This new life was to last another forty years. Did Moses embrace this dramatic turnabout in his life and fortunes, or did he merely accept it? The culture shock must have been intense.

> "Jethro [Reuel], Moses' father-in-law, together with Moses' sons and wife, came to him in the wilderness, where he was camped near the mountain of God. . . . Jethro was delighted to hear about all the good things the LORD had done for Israel. . . . He said, 'Praise be to the LORD, who rescued you from the hand of the Egyptians and Pharaoh. . . . Now I know that the LORD is greater than all other gods. . . . Then Jethro . . . brought a burnt offering and other sacrifices to God, and Aaron came with all the elders of Israel to eat a meal with Moses' father-in-law in the presence of God."
>
> Exodus 18:5, 9–12

Backtracking to pick up the narrative thread, Moses had sent his wife and sons back to her father during the early days of the Israelites' exodus journey. Currently the Israelites are encamped at Mount Sinai. Jethro, along with Moses's wife and sons, travels to Sinai to meet with the Israelites prior to the first organized stage of their journey. The intention is for Jethro to deliver Moses's family before returning home, alone, to Midian. This visit indicates not only that they remained on amicable terms but that the throng hadn't been hard for the Midianites to locate.

"The next day Moses took his seat to serve as judge for the people, and they stood around him from morning till evening. . . . Moses' father-in-law replied, 'What you are doing is not good. You and these people who come to you will only wear yourselves out. The work is too heavy for you; you cannot handle it alone. . . . Select capable men from all the people—men who fear God, trustworthy men who hate dishonest gain—and appoint them as officials over thousands, hundreds, fifties and tens.' . . . Then Moses sent his father-in-law on his way, and Jethro returned to his own country."

Exodus 18:13, 17–18, 21, 27

Jethro's concern about Moses's overextending himself is touching; it also feels contemporary to our often frenetic twenty-first-century pace. God's concern for us as people includes our vulnerability to burnout—a universal problem. "For he knows how we are formed, he remembers that we are dust" (Psalm 103:14). Moses's strength might have held out had he continued going it alone in lieu of delegating, but the God who values people cared enough to bring Jethro into the picture to mediate the situation with a word of fatherly wisdom. Encounters like this are never random with God. He appoints just the right people and circumstances to meet us in our times of need.

21

THE SYROPHOENICIAN WOMAN

"Jesus withdrew to the region of Tyre and Sidon. A Canaanite woman from that vicinity came to him, crying out, 'Lord, Son of David, have mercy on me! My daughter is demon-possessed and suffering terribly.' Jesus did not answer a word. So his disciples came to him and urged him, 'Send her away, for she keeps crying out after us.' He answered, 'I was sent only to the lost sheep of Israel.' The woman came and knelt before him. 'Lord, help me!' she said. He replied, 'It is not right to take the children's bread and toss it to the dogs.' 'Yes it is, Lord,' she said. 'Even the dogs eat the crumbs that fall from their master's table.' Then Jesus said to her, 'Woman, you have great faith! Your request is granted.'"

Matthew 15:21–28

"Jesus . . . went to the vicinity of Tyre. He entered a house and did not want anyone to know it; yet he could not keep his presence secret. In fact, as soon as she heard about him, a woman whose little daughter was possessed by an impure spirit came and fell at his feet. The woman was a Greek, born in Syrian Phoenicia. She begged Jesus to drive the demon out of her daughter. 'First let the children eat all they want,' he told her, 'for it is not right to take the children's bread and toss it to the dogs.' 'Lord,' she replied, 'even the dogs under the table eat the children's crumbs.' Then he told her, 'For such a reply, you may go; the demon has left your daughter.'"

Mark 7:14–30

Pertinent Scriptures: **Matthew 15:21–28; Mark 7:14–30**

Matthew and Mark tell the story differently, but the gist is the same. Matthew had been an eyewitness, while John Mark had learned the story from Peter, who had verbalized his recollection of the event. The differing nuances are helpful.

Jesus's approach to the woman catches us off guard. We know that his primary mission was to Israel and that he was exhausted and possibly on edge at this point. Mark's account brings out Jesus's desire for anonymity. Galilee at the time was a hotbed of opposition for him, and he desired private time for teaching his disciples. The trip to Tyre was intended to allow him a chance to regroup and reconnect.

The disconnect comes in that we wouldn't expect Jesus to be cryptic in his dealings with people, let alone caustic! Our lack of experience with sinlessness doesn't allow us to gauge the effect fatigue might have had on Jesus. Could this human experience have caused him to be ill-equipped to respond empathically? This is a question we lack the capacity to answer.

It does seem as though Jesus's apparent baiting of the woman was a test—and that she felt emboldened to play along. Considering the status of women, and of Gentiles, in the eyes of Jewish males, we are surprised at her audacity, . . . until we realize that she was at the end of her tether. As Jodi Picoult observes, "The desperate usually succeed because they have nothing to lose."

Was this woman's tenacity in character for her, or was it the result of despairing mother love? What this foreigner lacked was entitlement. She had no "right" to Jesus's help and knew it; yet she had an immediate need that overrode this restriction. In some sense it even overrode the strictures of common decency; clearly Jesus was tired and needed space.

None of that mattered at this moment; her daughter needed help—*now!*—and no other consideration mattered. Did she really consider herself, or her suffering child, a dog under the table salivating in its eagerness to scarf up the children's crumbs? At the least, she rightly considered her argument difficult to circumvent. As the mother of a desperately needy child (think of the ferocity of a bear protecting her cubs), she couldn't afford to be intimidated.

Jesus was impressed with her degree of faith, her intuitive understanding of who he was (her acknowledgment of Jesus as "Lord" happens only here in the book of Mark), her ready wit, and her humility. We might question this last point based on her bold rejoinder, but when we consider her willingness to settle for crumbs of grace, we can't help but be moved.

Given what we know of the submission expected of biblical women, we continue to be surprised by their pluck, their grit, and their capability. Jesus saw the intrinsic value of this mother and daughter and cared deeply, despite his disconcerting initial approach.

22

TAMAR ONE

"Judah recognized [his cord and staff] and said, 'She is more righteous than I, since I wouldn't give her to my son Shelah.' And he did not sleep with her again."
Genesis 38:26

"If brothers are living together and one of them dies without a son, his widow must not marry outside the family. Her husband's brother shall take her and marry her and fulfill the duty of a brother-in-law to her. The first son she bears shall carry on the name of the dead brother so that his name will not be blotted out from Israel."
Deuteronomy 25:5–6

Pertinent Scriptures: **Genesis 38; Deuteronomy 25:5–10; Mark 12:18–27**

❧

The sordid story shared in Genesis 38 is too complex for a brief summary. The detail may already be familiar, but a chapter readthrough will refresh the memory. Though Tamar's deed stuns us, it is hard to find fault with her intention. Judah himself recognized the rightness of her actions, given the circumstances. All three of Judah's sons were of Canaanite stock, as was Tamar. We know, however, that she was aware of the constricting rules surrounding levirate marriage delineated in Deuteronomy 25 but evidently already known during this earlier period. The detail in Deuteronomy 25:7–10 is so stark as to be truly alarming.

Why is this seemingly parenthetical incident included—almost intruded, it would seem—in salvation history? We aren't told, but we do note that this close-up of Judah provides a stark contrast to the character of Joseph. Ironically, the Old Testament includes two stories of Tamars, both of whom were sexually degraded in the worst of ways (see also 2 Samuel 13:1–30). The more difficult Old Testament stories are seldom tame and tend to be much more descriptive than suggestive. Too often such accounts are passed over as too hot to handle.

That double standard in the Genesis stories involving the treatment of men versus women comes to the fore. And the picture in some ways hasn't changed. A touch point may apply to us more as members of society than of families. Does our culture expect a higher standard of morality in women than in men? Are we quicker to excuse the grieving widower for sexual indiscretion than the woman with whom he is involved? Do we assume the woman is less driven by passion, better able to control her impulses, and therefore more accountable?

"Since we live in a world that relies on women to be tidy in all ways," observes Jaclyn Friedman, "to be quiet and obedient and agreeable and available (but never aggressive), those of us who color outside of the lines get called sluts. And that word is meant to keep us in line."

Joel Ryan makes the following observation: "Tamar and Judah later bore twin boys named Perez and Zerah. Ironically, out of Perez's line, both King David and later Jesus Christ, the Messiah, were born (Matthew 1:3). This is testament to God's prevailing mercy. For even the most flawed and sinful of men can be used and blessed by God, not because of their merit, but because of His grace and the power of repentance." What comfort does this observation give to each of us as we contemplate the long-suffering, unfailing forgiveness of our God, the lover of people!

23

TAMAR TWO

"In the course of time, Amnon son of David fell in love with Tamar, the beautiful sister of Absalom son of David. Amnon became so obsessed with his sister Tamar that he made himself ill. She was a virgin, and it seemed impossible for him to do anything to her."
2 Samuel 13:1–2

"'Go to bed and pretend to be ill,' Jonadab said. 'When your father comes to see you, say to him, "I would like my sister Tamar to come and give me something to eat. Let her prepare the food in my sight so I may watch her and then eat it from her hand."'"
2 Samuel 13:5

Amnon "refused to listen to her, and since he was stronger than she, he raped her. Then Amnon hated her with intense hatred. In fact, he hated her more than he had loved her. Amnon said to her, 'Get up and get out!' . . . Tamar put ashes on her head and tore the ornate robe she was wearing. She put her hands on her head and went away, weeping aloud as she went. . . . Tamar lived in her brother Absalom's house, a desolate woman."
2 Samuel 13:14–15, 19, 22

Pertinent Scripture: **2 Samuel 13:1–38**

❧

We have no way of knowing how much David's older children understood of what had transpired with Bathsheba and Uriah, but they must have surmised enough. It seems that David, following his conversation with Nathan, came to terms with his failings and their fallout. But residual guilt remained, along with a diminished sense of entitlement to discipline his children.

Amnon's scheme was anything but adroit; beyond arranging an opportunity to be alone with his half-sister, he wasted no energy in forethought. And the fact that he raped Tamar *because he could* does nothing for his reputation. His reaction to his victim following his assault is telling. Tamar's "accusing" presence posed an impediment to any positive prospects he could foresee.

Tamar's future was bleak, snuffed out in the cruelest manner at the prime of her young life. She had as yet experienced none of the exhilaration of young love. This unsuspecting princess went within the probable span of one-half hour from

"Come in!" to "Get out!"—with the door barred behind her. A poignant quote from Bertolt Brecht seems pertinent here: "The human race tends to remember the abuses to which it has been subjected rather than the endearments. What's left of kisses? Wounds, however, leave scars."

Two Old Testament Tamars—both disgraced in the most horrific manner (see also Genesis 38). One bringing the dishonor upon herself as a backhanded means to rectify years of neglect and broken promises, the other an unwilling participant, shamed by her half-brother's lust and then tossed aside like a dirty rag. The Old Testament minces no words when it comes to the kinds of stories that make us squirm. Ironically, our own society is hardly tight lipped; perhaps we can relate to these sordid stories in a way previous generations found difficult.

Joel Ryan comments on similarities between these accounts: "Two women, two stories. Both deal with the spiritual blindness of father figures and the spiritual corruption and moral failure of young men. Both stories reveal injustices towards women and explore the consequences of sexual sin upon families. But in both unusual accounts, the grace of God is on display for those willing to confess and repent from their sin."

In an insightful article on the second Tamar story, Dierdre Brour has this to say: "Tamar lived desolate, but her testimony does not end in desolation. Tamar's voice of wisdom and outrage continues to speak today. The biblical writers have honored and preserved her voice for those willing to listen. She offers life-giving sustenance through her words of wisdom and her outrage against evil. Tamar confronts evil with truth and speaks with authority on behalf of the narrator and the laws and wisdom of Israel. The narrator validates Tamar's voice and bears witness to the multidimensional violence, consequences, and devastation of rape. Amnon represents godless foolishness, while Tamar represents godly wisdom."

The consequences of this outrage included in the following chapters of 2 Samuel go far beyond what we might have expected. This spark of indiscretion ignited a firestorm the ramifications of which reach throughout the remainder of Old Testament history and into the New. God's consuming love transcends wickedness, validating Tamar's value—and that of all other abused image bearers—in his holy eyes.

24

URIAH

"In the spring, at the time when kings go off to war, David sent Joab out with the king's men and the whole Israelite army. . . . But David remained in Jerusalem. One evening David got up from his bed and walked around on the roof of the palace. From the roof he saw a woman bathing. The woman was very beautiful, and David sent someone out to find out about her. The man said, 'She is Bathsheba, the daughter of Eliam and the wife of Uriah the Hittite.'"

2 Samuel 11:1–3

"The woman conceived and sent word to David, saying, 'I am pregnant.' So David sent word to Joab: 'Send me Uriah the Hittite.' . . . When Uriah came to him, David asked him how Joab was, how the soldiers were and how the war was going. Then David said to Uriah, 'Go down to your house and wash your feet.' . . . But Uriah slept at the entrance to the palace. . . . David . . . asked Uriah, 'Haven't you just come from a military campaign? Why didn't you go home?' Uriah said to David, 'The ark and Israel and Judah are staying in tents, and my commander Joab and my lord's men are camped in the open country. How could I go to my house to eat and drink and make love to my wife?'"

2 Samuel 11:5–11

"In the morning David wrote a letter to Joab and sent it with Uriah. In it he wrote, 'Put Uriah out in front where the fighting is fiercest. Then withdraw from him so he will be struck down and die.' . . . Joab sent David a full account of the battle. He instructed the messenger: 'When you have finished giving the king this account of the battle, the king's anger may flare up, and he may ask you, 'Why did you get so close to the city to fight?' . . . If he asks you this, then say to him, 'Moreover, your servant Uriah the Hittite is dead.'"

2 Samuel 11:14–21

Pertinent Scripture: **2 Samuel 11:1–12:14**

❦

We know that Uriah was a soldier in David's army, but few of us realize that he was part of the exclusive, elite corps of only thirty-seven at the time (2 Samuel 23:39) known as his Mighty Men; think of the status of the Navy Seals but on a much smaller scale. These principled soldiers were close cohorts of David who had stuck with him during the difficult years before his kingship was established and had sacrificed much to ensure the king's welfare. Not to mention, in Uriah's case, that he lived "next door" to the palace.

As discussed in the chapter on Ephron, the Hittites were a people group descended from Noah. They lived in Canaan, and their religion was pluralistic. Due to their despicable pagan practices, the post-exodus Israelites were called upon to annihilate them and the post-exilic Israelites to avoid intermarriage with them.

Uriah was likely a descendant of Hittites who had lived in the land since the time of Abraham and had by this point been accepted as Israelites. He was evidently a God-fearer who was not officially a part of the Hittite nation, since Gentile status would have prevented his marriage to Bathsheba.

Nathan's memorable confrontation of David over the arranged murder of Uriah (2 Samuel 12:1–13), including the convicting parable David initially failed to apply to himself, makes for compelling reading. It took Nathan's cryptic "You are the man!" for David to finally face his guilt and concede, "I have sinned against the LORD." First Kings 15:5 offers a cryptic summation of David's life: "David had done what was right in the eyes of the LORD and had not failed to keep any of the LORD's commands all the days of his life—except in the case of Uriah the Hittite." By extension, we can include in this exception David's adultery with Uriah's wife.

David wrote Psalm 51 shortly after his confrontation by Nathan, and it is worth a read with this context in mind. God's indictment through Nathan was biting (2 Samuel 12:7–11), but upon David's admission of guilt the prophet was quick to go on, "The LORD has taken away your sin. You are not going to die. But because by doing this you have shown contempt for the LORD, the son born to you will die.'"

It is surprising that Uriah's name is mentioned in Matthew's genealogy of Jesus: "David was the father of Solomon, whose mother had been Uriah's wife" (Matthew 1:6). Along with Matthew's inclusion of three Gentile women in the lineup (Tamar, Rahab, and Ruth), this nod to Uriah may have been a subtle way for Matthew, writing to a Jewish audience, to make a point about God's inclusivity.

Uriah makes only a brief appearance in the chronology of the Bible and is a minor player in David and Bathsheba's story, but his legacy is honorable. There can be no question of God's valuation of this God-fearer. The meaning of Uriah's name: "Yahweh is my light"!

25

THE WIDOW OF ZAREPHATH

"Some time later the brook dried up because there had been no rain in the land. Then the word of the LORD came to [Elijah]: 'Go at once to Zarephath in the region of Sidon and stay there. I have directed a widow there to supply you with food.' . . . When he came to the town gate, a widow was there gathering sticks. He called to her and asked, 'Would you . . . bring me, please, a piece of bread.' 'As surely as the LORD your God lives,' she replied, 'I don't have any bread—only a handful of flour in a jar and a little olive oil in a jug.' . . . Elijah said to her, 'Don't be afraid. Go home and do as you have said. But first make a small loaf of bread for me from what you have and bring it to me, and then make something for yourself and your son. For this is what the LORD, the God of Israel, says: "The jar of flour will not be used up and the jug of oil will not run dry until the day the LORD sends rain on the land."'"

1 Kings 17:7–14

"A father to the fatherless, a defender of widows, is God in his holy dwelling."

Psalm 68:5

Pertinent Scripture: **1 Kings 17:7–24**

There's an interesting play on the subject of death in this tightly woven two-act story, reflected by the widow's words to Elijah: "I am gathering a few sticks to take home and make a meal for myself and my son, that we may eat it—*and die*" and later "What do you have against me, man of God? Did you come to remind me of my sin and *kill my son*?" (emphasis added in both quotes).

It seems incredible that this widow, a foreigner, would be so willing to trust the prophet—or his God—as to feed him first, before herself and her son. We could pass this off as courtesy, as resignation, or even as a forcing of the inevitable, with her assuming that this would have been her family's final meal.

"Some time later the son of the woman who owned the house became ill. He grew worse and worse, and finally stopped breathing. . . . The LORD heard Elijah's cry, and the boy's life returned to him, and he lived. . . . Then the woman said to Elijah, 'Now I know that you are a man of God and that the word of the LORD from your mouth is the truth.'"

1 Kings 17:17, 22, 24

49

It's the boy's later death that strikes us as a disconnect. *Where did this come from?* we want to ask. This unforeseen loss *following* the miraculous survival of mother and son must have seemed the ultimate in capricious cruelty—some sort of sadistic "divine comedy," perhaps not unexpected had the source been a god like Sidon's. This distraught mother might never have recognized the ramifications of God's reward for faithfulness had not this second miracle showcased his power and goodness.

I'm reminded by this story of the New Testament account of the widow putting her last two copper coins into the temple treasury (Mark 12:41–44). Jesus's words on that occasion resonate here: "Truly I tell you, this poor widow has put more into the treasury than all the others. They all gave out of their wealth; but she, out of her poverty, put in everything—all she had to live on."

The plight of the widow from Sidon was even more immediate. The small loaf she had planned to bake would have been the last physical sustenance for herself and her son she could foresee. "The most sublime act," reflects William Blake, "is to set another before you." Once again, we see that supreme sacrifice coming from a non-Israelite. And once again God was intimately acquainted with her situation and cared deeply enough to perform a second miracle to ensure that she recognized and received the message of his love.

Contents for Characters of the Bible Series: Book 1

Flawed Bible Characters
and the God Who Chooses, Uses, and Loves

Contents for Characters of the Bible Series: Book 3

Wicked Bible Characters and the God Who Works His Sovereign Plan